# The rime of MIA & the WOLF

Ashley Barker

The rime of Mia & the Wolf
First published in 2026
koniecpress@gmail.com



ISBN 978-83-979574-0-4

for M

# ARGUMENT

Five-year-old Mia wakes in the night and finds herself alone.

The wolf under her parents' bed is coaxed out with a tear. He promises to stay until Mia's mother returns - and for once is as good as his word.

*

Fixed then broken
Wolf drops to dust
abandoning ship
abandoning us.

Equally leaky
Wolf, woman and child
in different directions
set sail
                    for
                              The Wild.

1.

When I woke
I broke night's silence.
Mummy, I said
to Mummy's absence.

The landing-light stream
across my bed,
my door and I
left a river in flood.

I found the living room
dead and cold,
the plugs unplugged,
the curtains pulled.

The kitchen was dark,
and the kettle I must *never*
*ever* reach for or touch,
its cold touch made me shiver.

Opening Mummy's wardrobe,
Daddy's coat was still there:
long, grey and lost,
lying crumpled on the floor (the coat he wore
washing up on Mummy's shore).

No footprints in the snow,
neither from nor to our door...
I stood tiptoe at the window,
watching snow cocoon our car.

I looked under Mummy's bed,
and the wolf, he looked back at me.
"Are we alone?" he said (said amber eyes),
"Only two, when we should be three?"

A tear told him what I couldn't say,
then like a genie from a lamp,
out he came, my wolf, to play,
all smelly, grey, and damp.

He lifted his head and *howled,* he did,
and *howwww-llll,* I did too.
Wolf's howl spoke of things impossible
to put into words, just now, for you.

When we'd finished howling -
the silence more silent than before
- "Mummy will be home soon," said the wolf.
"Til then, Wolfcub, I'm yours.

"So up!" he said. So up I climbed.
"Hold fast!" he said, then *whoooosh!*
The ducked-under frame of the bedroom door
went past with a gasp, in a flash.

We flew down the stairs in leaps and bounds
into darkness, fearless. "*Faster!*"
  The baying for blood of shadowy hounds
at our heels, drowned out by laughter.

Out through the kitchen - "CHAAAAARGE!"
- backdoor banging, pots and pans a-ding-dong;
me in PJs and slippers in the snow
with a wolf who'd not a stitch on.

Mummy, if she'd seen us - good grief!
- would've raged and dragged me to bed,
and the wolf, in the moment's heat,
would've shown his teeth,
every tooth in his head
(regret what he'll swear he never said
did
had...).

Glum in the glow of a Christmas tree,
limbs unlit, loaded low with snow ...

Wolf butts the trunk, starts an avalanche,
and plays the bucking bronco.

The backyard left (in clouds of breath),
hearthside, by glowing embers,
between two hefty paws the blood's
huffed back into my fingers.

It's then a need takes hold of me.
"TEE-VEEEE!" I demand, "TEE-VEEEE!" I plead.
   "Switch it on," says the wolf. "Seriously:
fire up that thing, I leave.

"I'll not plant nightmare seeds.
There are things this late you're not to see.
And your ma ... 'll be rightly angry,
she gets back you're watching TV!"

Simply, "Wolf," I say,
"please let me."

Whatever's a wolf to do?
- put down his paw,
lay down the law,
defy his puppeteer?

(She knows who her little finger's for
does wolfish Mia.)
He'll play it by pricked ear.
"Five minutes," he says.

"You hear? No more.
She comes through that front door ...!
kiss our hides goodbye
seven strides or fewer.
"But, hey.

"I'm game if you are."

Half an hour ticks past
grimly lit in the grip
of the horribly bad
*Zombie Pirates: War Ship*

Wolf shielding my eyes
(well, he tries)
and my ears
from what he thinks for me unfit.

A hairy-digit-filtered slit
allows an Arrgh!
elicits Eeek!
is shut at "*SHHHH**!*    Sorry."

Wolf tickled, giggles, grins,
blurts worse - his Huh?
answered, "Mummy?"...

Ten miles below Wolf
plops Wolf's skin.

*Mummy* announced to something,
nothing, a distant storm I imagine.

Wolf takes no chances, pounces,
kills the television.

We wait together, sat in darkness
healed as soon as broken,
Mia's wolf and wolfcub Mia,
dreading thunder, ears wide open -

ready            set

waiting in the blocks for a pop. Instead
each sound's misread. All. All
false starts, our nerves
in shreds. A fox,

a cat nags at the trigger,
the settling house, a change of weather
- the night's full repertoire
's *yer mother.*
                                        Only not in the flesh. Not her.

                                                        Him neither.

Him (half the danger
apparently passed): "Sit back," speak teeth,
spark teeth in the dark. "Battle *axed.*"

Those teeth again, Daddy's laugh.

"Where is she," I ask, "so late at night?
Out looking for you?"
Wolf hangs his head. I see a star
that won't be shed or hid.

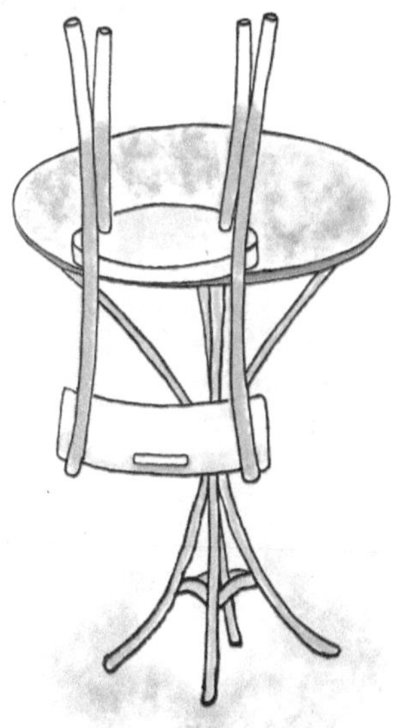

"All the wolves," he says.

"All the wolves of the forest ..."
(The wind drops, cocks an ear,
drops so especially to hear.)

"All the wolves of the forest
howl their hardest for this
- for a kiss, an embrace, to be face to face
with the ones they've so missed.

"I know *exactly* where that ma of yours is.

"She's on her way back here, that's where.
Because here *you* are, that's why.
No storm, no zombie-pirate crew
could come between your ma and you.

"You're the grey-blue apple of her eye."

"And in brown?

What am I, in pale brown eyes?"

"Everything you hear. The lies, the truth.
The truth," he decides,
my wolf in disguise.

"Come," he says. "Come here. Come close."
And he curls himself around me.
"It's late. We'll wait together."

"You'll wait with me? - for Mummy?"

The smile is slow to leave my lips. S l o w e d
down I go, into the depths
of a well-known smelly heat. I slip
and snuggle down to sleep, from "Yes."

'Yes' is all, is a rope-lashed wheel,
'Yes' shifts the house to an even keel
as a dreamed-up ocean fills the garden,
spills from *Yes, I will*'s horizon.

We put to sea with all the speed
the breath of *Yes, I will* allows,
from an island harbour once known as
the booming hills above our house.

And although the words
that stirred the sails
rolled from a mouth
whose words had failed us

miserably in the past
(or so I've heard),
I nail his colours
to my mast.

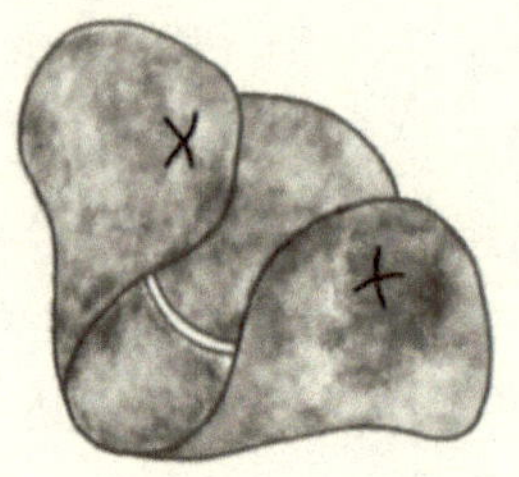

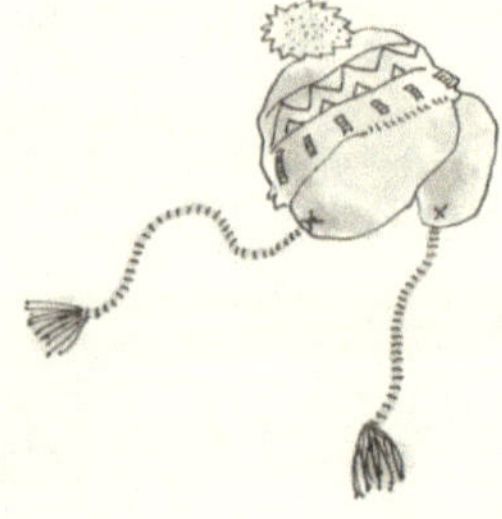

**

Wind whips down sleet
and whips up waves.
On a petal a needle
pitches, whirls.

TIE UP THOSE SHEETS!
BATTEN DOWN THOSE HATCHES!
Hold on to your seats.

Let fly your HAT*SEZZZZZZ!*

2.

A bad-dream zombie pirate ship
gains ground up-down mountainous seas,
chasing the house to storm its walls
and plunder as they please.

("I've a *wolf.*
Think again, zombies.")

Soon hard alongside
(skittling the trash),
zombies board, maraud,
they swagger and gush

like a wave down the hall,
up the stairs with the rats.
At the glass wall of "*Hushhhh!*"
at my door they collapse.

Lips sealed with a claw
part to white.
"Mia sleeps," says the wolf.
"You double the fight

you wake her up."
He stands his full height.
"Back away," he says. "*Now.*
I won't tell you twice."

Wolf feints a lunge,
starts a domino effect
from the first to the next,
the last zombie on deck.

With a clatter of cutlasses,
muskets and knives,
Wolf flattens the crew,
their imp children and wives,

stays dry in a rain of bullets and blades
(has the size of 10 cats
x 10 cats
x 9 lives).

Zombies upped with their anchor,
twenty-plus in a chain,
drop back from Wolf's snarl
and his snap to the waves.

To the rap-a-tap bones
of a retreat-beating drummer,
over soft groans of gangplanks
threatening to crack,

to The Bad Ship Carbuncle -
planks gables to gunwales
- in a conga, a shuffle,
scared zombies edge back.

"Is that all you've *got?*" yells I - too soon.
Zombie cannons BOOM! BOOM!
in reply, shoot the moon
from the sky,

send a skittering of bricks
down the roof, down the chimney,
and some sort of fairy
shot down passing by.

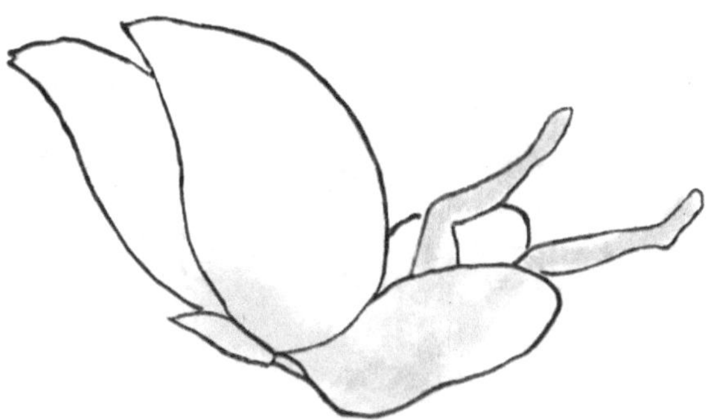

Zombies brought to their senses
by the mess, all these ashes,
the poor fairy, the damage,
fear of The Tongue (forty lashes),

slowly but surely
catch a stiff whiff of victory -
an aroma unfamiliar, sweet and sour,
sweet and sickly.

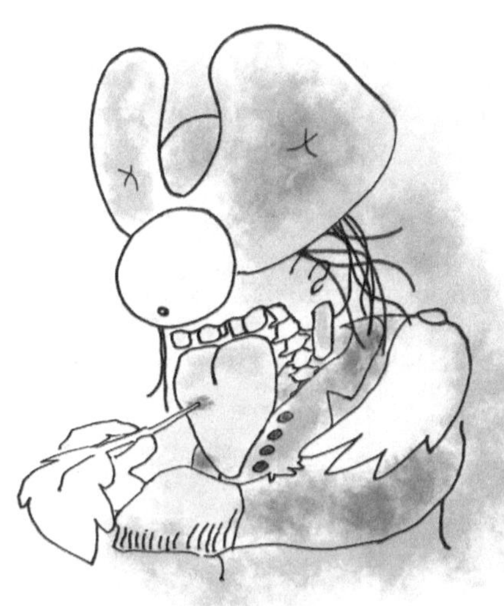

Drunk captain, a cyclops,
a mute with a quill:
"WITH THIS SHIP AT OUR MERCY,"
he scribbles, "WE PAUSE?????"

Tongue like a necktie,
with no lower jaw,
in 9-inch-high capital letters
he RRROOOAAAAAARRRS!

His roars ignite more
zombie roars til the room
is a furnace of noise -
tender ears would've bled.

Asides Wolf: "This'll not end well,
I promise," he says.
"It's lucky for them
they're already dead.

"SWABS WANNA PLAY *ROUGH?*
Gloves off! Let's PLAY!"
Wolf spits out a tooth
(not his, by the way)

and leaps into battle.
The eye of the fray
becomes Wolf and the fairy
shot down, who's okay -

*believed in* (the main thing),
if not quite recovered.

Back to back - a winged wolf
- they take on all-comers

from starboard to doll's house,
port to toy cupboard.
But for each zombie felled
appear two, three, four others

lumbering up to replace
the ones planted facewards or
backwards or buckled at the knees
to the floorboards

- while the Capt'n
one eye on a deadly position
drops books from the shelves
scaled (sobered) like rigging

to wait like a hunter
a vulture, tongue dripping
the Fairy Conduct hotline
in a gold-ringed ear ringing...

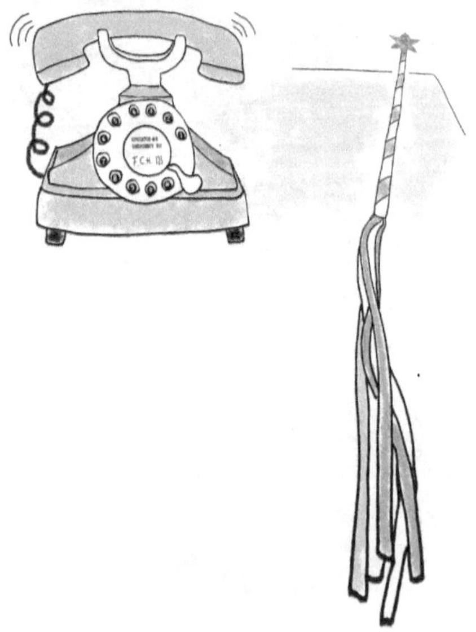

Of the tooth-gathering type
        fighting not in her nature
grassed up, the poor fairy
        wings scarce fit to carry her

disembarks with black marks
        earned for courage, for valour
reported for fighting
        why and whom not the matter

leaving Wolf naughty-cornered
        black marks off the chart
behind a curled-fist wall of
a-twitch body parts

v a deepening ditch
o′ vile blaggards in bits
        - if bit moves, on it fights
much too dead now to quit.

At the elbow, the shoulder,
the hip, neck, the wrist,
zombies snap like old twigs -
all it takes's a quick twist,

a smart wrench, the last stitch
pops or rips, slips its mooring.
"This hits," says the wolf, of the wall,
"ride it in! Wake'll take you to morning."

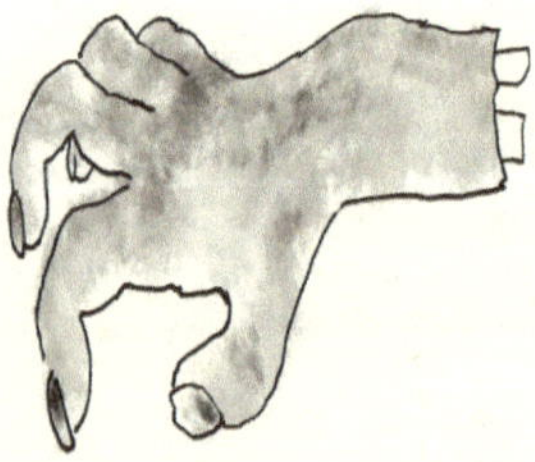

Zombie heap, as we speak
(Wolf busy dismembering),
if I stood on its ridge,
within reach of the ceiling.

I ask him, "And you?...
And where you going?"
I'm asking and asking, politely,
then screaming:

"BLOODY ANSWER MY QUESTION!"
  Wolf turning a deaf 'un;
from a broken toy pram
he's fashioned a weapon.

To the enemy, at length,
his whole length Wolf presents.
"This is yours, not their dance,"
is at last his response

- stepping out of the game,
the above to announce at great pains...

The Zombie Cap'n, squinting, cranes,
takes aim,
                                        cuts in all the same.

***

Taught to sit
and stay
with hackles
          raised

tail between legs
          to whine, beg
          play nice
          play dead.

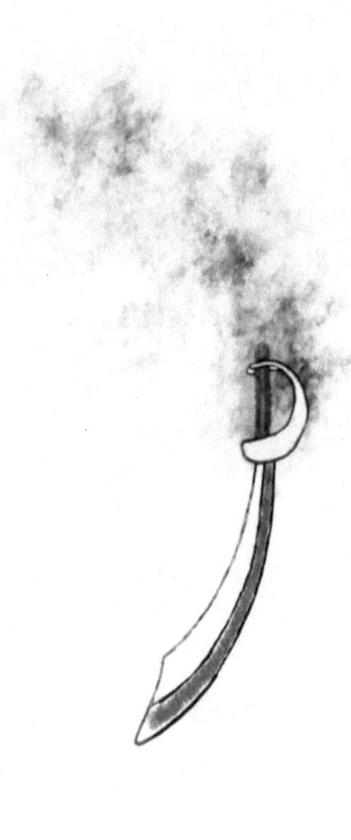

3.

Wolf draws on the cutlass
like north would a compass,
its needle tugged heartwards,
to sadness, a weakness.

From one to the other,
the sword to Wolf's chest,
spans Time - the blink of an eye
at best - all the time a grain less.

Mia finds, against Time,
that the more she protests
the thicker the treacle
Time has to turn in.

Clocks thicken their ticking
to barely a trickle
and slow the blade's progress -
a shot from a pistol

'd be slowed to a dawdle.

Mid-air the blade twinkles
like a slow-turning crystal,
stays true to its path

like soup, dentists, baths,
school, helping Out About the House
Now You're Not Quite So Small
- inescapable, all
                                        inescapable.

But a tantrum, in truth,
can only steamroll Time thin;
all ahead still looms large -
what's coming is coming,

written in cloud-topped
grey blocks of carved stone,
every future mistake chiseled deep,
packed with bone.

Done wheeling, toothed cutlass
scrape-thunks its way home,
and that's where it stops,
as far as it's thrown.

****

However much expected
it still comes as a shock:
Mummy's key, waking me,
twisting painfully in the lock

(freeing each and every clock.
   Sparking, squealing red-hot cogs
race, breast the tape, sedately tick-tock
poker-faced).

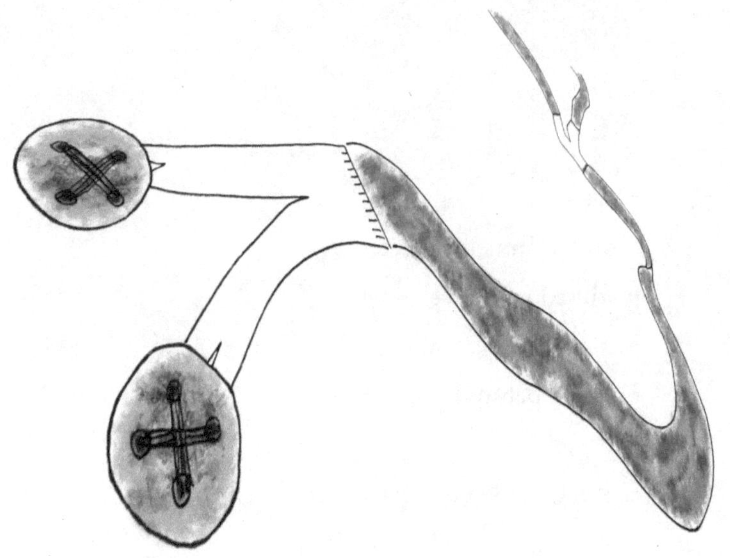

4.

White knuckled, baring teeth ...

Uprooted from sleep - being dragged
shoulder-deep down a heel-dug furrow
- Mia loosed Time's arrow.

With a whiplashing crack,
Time's braces snap back
from drawn lips, knotted nose...
Mummy, paused by its echo,

fancies Wolf in the shadows
(that glorified mutt and his Alpha act,
shutting up the stairs' pack
of hounds' yip-yap).

Off she pads, on her rounds
with a baseball bat - timid, on the attack
- the squeak of barefeet from
front door to back.

Downstairs, at least,
not a peep to report -
groundfloor windows, back door,
found sound and secure.

Then that sound that she'd heard
she hears it anew - a brave big-hand twitch
does the trick. "It was you!"
- a smirking eight minutes to two

(a dour twenty to four -
take your pick of the hour
- every racing clock just stopped where it was,
wherever they were,

at one with the cause
if not quite with each other.

In hushed, snippy voices:
"Oh look. Mia's mother."

"So it is! Well, I never!"
"What time's she call this?"
"High time!"
"Any time she chooses!"

- each clock pulling one
of six different faces.
"She'll never notice," the most accurate
clock in the house says).

Shadow hounds lick her hands
as she climbs darkened stairs,
mouth and paw. Not a snore
reaches Mummy at my door.

Nothing more than before
follows, "Mia?..." spoken twice.
  On goes the light.            Mummy drops
through a 60-watt crack in the ice.

(Wolf would like to be nice,
lie that line: *It's alright,*
hold her close, whisper, "Chloé..."

   She'd get the fright of her life,

batter him OUT! OUT! OUT! side.
He'd take the hiding rather than hide,
not shy of agony, any
cutting down to size: fine,

done wordlessly.
"Swords, sticks or stones'll never hurt me,"
grins the wolf, gap-toothed,
lamed, bloodied.)

Off the flame til now, comes Mummy.
Mummy, seeking - warmer, warmer
- beholds the wardrobe - hot - 's *got* to be:
stashed away, snug in a corner,

her daughter in the doldrums - *Ho!*
the little mutineer - below dead sails,
a swaybacked rail's worth of (not)
not-a-thing-to-wear.

*Look alive. Your mother's here.*

*Seven... Six ... Five ...*

Trailed by kittens she arrives;
from my side slopes the wolf
- an eye on them both, though my eyes
are closed.                    Fine comes. Foul goes.

Head sunk, full of holes (on zero
- howling 'O's), into my ears and up my nose
Mummy's scent and sobbing grows, explodes
                    with a flash
as sails
        return
        to clothes.

*****

One day
- one night, more likely -
on pussycat toes, quieter
than quietly

I'll follow my wolf down
to his lair. ("Oh yeah? That's ...
You're funny. That's a beaut.
Over my dead body.            Real cute.")

5.

A shoulder-damaged suit
and an age-yellowed dress
in cahoots, chest-to-chest,
guard a silk-lined nest.

To my name I'm deaf, or,
hearing it, mute,
then in one fell swoop,
parting dress from suit ...

Amid old bad smells,
tangled sandals, thorny heels,
a swept-back wedding dress reveals
    [cue tinkling clapperless bells]

a flawed-perfect pearl,
a 'silly' sleep-wrecked girl,
bed-headed, in tears.
There she is

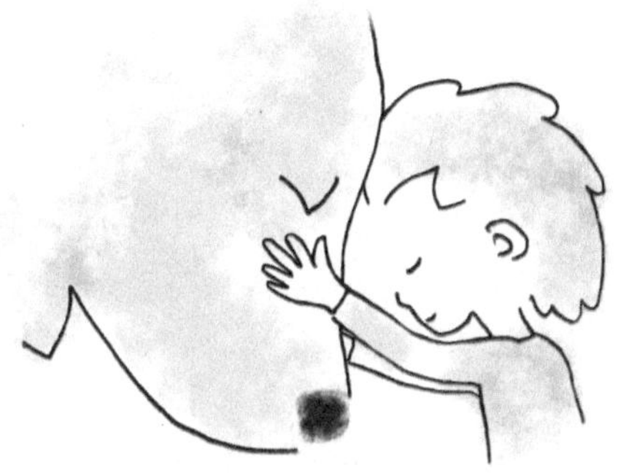

there, at a stroke,
still afloat, chin to knees
on Daddy's old, grey, smelly coat,
held tightly in its sleeves. Held

*tightly* in its sleeves. Held tight.
"Sweet dreams, Wolfcub," Wolf breathes.
"G'night.
Don't Let Those
Zombies
Bite."

******

Goodnight? G′morning, more like
- light fat behind the blinds,
each slat a dirty line.
Wolf pleads, mouths, mimes

(from earshot gone
then gone from sight and smell. From smell ...
*not quite*): "DON'T
(let those) ZOMBIES
BITE!"

I Wont

6.

"I WON'T!" I shout,
right into her ear.
Mummy's lifting me up,
on her knees, when I'm steered

somewhere soft and half-dropped
half-placed to the floor
and left.                    Refusing to slam,
the bedroom door heaves a breath.

Left face-to-face
with what's under the bed
where it's hid, all there is
all he had that was his

here I am
milktooth-to-fang with
books, papers, discs
a few clothes

things that showed
empty shelves' worth of tat
leaving holes
Daddy's crap

Daddy's useless best stuff
boxed and taped
furred with dust

wolf-shaped -

when needs must

- wolf skin and bones
in a trap that, should I yawn,
'll yawn back
maw-to-maw

lift the bed
on the jack of its jaws (two, three legs in the air
- for a moment, all four)
without a sound.

Sensing uproar he'll soon
set the bed down, leave moons
on the wax of the marks made before
on scrubbed boards.
(No shoes allowed.
No claws.)

To put Wolf at ease:

"Oh, that bite?...
I just might."

His tail gets a squeeze.

"In they breeze

next scurvied
shipload of zombies?
Just might, Wolf.
Just might."

*The terrible tease.*

Boots vagabond brogues on a bag
that my jokes however bad
had not once failed to please
freeze.

Not hearing her come in
Mummy lies on the rug
on her side of the bed
gently slides Wolf's head
off his spine
so her eyes can meet mine.

When I find them, her eyes
are a she-wolf's, cried red

and they smile
almost speak, but nothing needs
to be said, so we meet
beneath bedspread

and blankets and sheets
and hug.                    We hug, almost laugh,
and that woolen, pooled plaid of a tail -
Daddy's scarf - gives a wag

and those tired-out brogues
both soles
heel to toe
untack

and a long turned-back tongue
lolls through the gap
grinning
like a maniac.

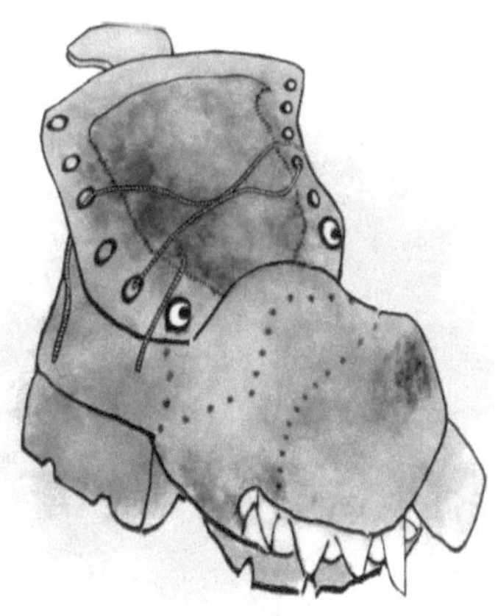

And that's that.

x

n.b.

Chances are you knew this by now, but no AI was used to write or illustrate this book. Its inevitable overlooked imperfections are entirely human.

A.

Ashley Barker's writing has appeared in many literary journals and on the London Fringe and Off-West End.

www.ingramcontent.com/pod-product-compliance
Lightning Source LLC
LaVergne TN
LVHW051015080826
845145LV00009B/2639

* 9 7 8 8 3 9 7 9 5 7 4 0 4 *